Eva's Inspirations

Inspired by God

Eva Dimel

Copyright 2015
By
Eva Dimel

ISBN 978-1-940609-41-6
Soft cover

All rights reserved
No part of this book may be reproduced or transmitted in any form or by any means, electronic or mechanical, including photocopying, recording, or by any information storage and retrieval system, without permission in writing from the copyright owner.

This book was printed in the United States of America.

To order additional copies of this book contact:

Eva Dimel
Phone -614-875-9263
EDimel9775@sbcglobal.net

Published by
FWB Publications
Columbus, Ohio

FWB

Eva Dimel

Dedication

I Would Like To Dedicate This Book To My Precious Mom, With Love.

Who Is Now Watching Over Me From Heaven

Preface

I pray this book is a blessing
To whoever reads it.
And that it touches your heart in so many ways.
Always with all the glory going to God,
For without
His inspiration I could not write anything.
God Bless You

Eva Dimel

A Day With God

Dear God, I've thought of all the blessings that you have sent my way,

And then I realized that I don't need anything today.

I just want to take the time to praise your Holy name,

And I want to thank you God, because of you my life has changed.

I want to thank you for each day knowing you are always there,

I want to take the time to show everyone that I love, just how much I care.

I want to enjoy all of the beauty that you have created for me,

And I pray that others will also take the time to see.

I want to share your love, and all your joy with others,

Reaching out a helping hand, to my sisters, and my brothers.

I want to take the time to stop and smell all the beautiful flowers,

And let time go by without worrying, how late or what's the hour.

I want to look up at the sky gazing at all the beautiful clouds,

And just sit and talk to you from my heart for a little while.

I want to just run freely through all the fresh green grass,

Not worrying about tomorrow, or what happened in the past.

I want to laugh and be silly until my sides are sore,

Filled with hope and wonder, thinking about what you have for me in store.

I want to let your love, and your peace, just fill my soul,

Thanking you for all your blessings that every day I see unfold.

And when my day is over and finally comes to an end,

Before I close my eyes to sleep I want to thank you once again.

A Happy Ending

For every storm that hits your life and every trial that you go through,

There's a happy ending waiting for God has promised this for you.

Though you may not see the rainbow and feel the sun shine on your face,

It is right there waiting for you God puts everything in place.

When you question and you wonder why me Lord every day,

Look up you're not alone God changes lives in every way.

As you're walking through the valley thinking this will never end,

Behold there stands your Father with a happy ending for you again.

Night time doesn't last forever and the sun will always rise,

You'll feel joy and you'll have laughter as the tears fade from your eyes.

Everyday things will get better as your life begins to change,

For every second every moment God will get you through the pain.

Take Gods hand and hold on tight as your journey in life begins,

Grateful to be with your Father knowing every happy ending comes from Him.

A Soldiers Dream

Quietly he stood on foreign land,

Geared up for battle with a gun in his hand.

Sleeping in places he had never been,

Praying he never had to sleep there again.

Eating whatever could be packed away,

Asking God to please keep him safe today.

He wondered why this even had to be,

God created us all and we were meant to be free.

There were so many lives lost, and broken hearts,

He knew he had to fight and do his part.

His family was always on his mind,

He loved them so much and prayed they'd be fine.

With his head held high he began to walk,

Looking up to God grateful they could talk.

Whatever happens God please watch over me,

So I can make it home to the land of the free.

I want to hug my family and hold them close,

And appreciate the things that mean the most.

This journey has taught me so much it seems,

I don't need a lot God, to fulfill this soldiers dream.

All Because Of You God

Some people say I have nothing but I know I do,

Dear God I know that it's all because of you.
I'm not very rich in silver or gold,

But I have riches to get me through my life, even when I am old.

I have family and friends, and I have love enough to share,

And a Father who is loving and for me is always there.

I have been forgiven of all of my sins,

And the chance to start my life all over again

I have blessings that I see in my life every day,

And a God who always hears me each time I pray.

My riches are of the most important kind,

They cannot be bought they are all free you will find.

Some people say I have nothing but I know I do,

I have everything I need God, and it's all because of you.

Always Asking

Always asking yes God that is me,

For you are the only hope in my life I see.

Always needing something from you,

Because you are the one who knows what to do.

Always questioning why so many trials, But you always show me they only last a short while.

Always wanting my answers today,

But you have shown me it doesn't happen that way.

Always worrying about things I can't change,

When I give it to you, you never complain.

Always wondering which road to take,

Knowing with you there are no mistakes.

Always thinking what am I worth, And you let me know I have loved you from birth.

Always trying to step into tomorrow,

While you hold me back saving me from extra sorrows.

Always I run to you all of the time,

Knowing you will take care of me and I will be fine.

Always asking for you're the one that I trust, My God my Father, the one who loves me so much.

Back Again

I was at the door wondering if I should even go in,

I could not believe I was back here again.

I thought everything was fine and my problems were gone,

But here I was again I was so wrong.

I knew He was waiting and expecting me,

He was my only hope and the one that I need.

As I called out His name the tears started to fall,

Like a river over flowing I couldn't handle it all.

The pain and the trials, and the sadness and fears,

Brought me to my Father I knew I'd be safe here.

Suddenly I felt His loving embrace,

Peace in my soul and strength for the things I must face.

I poured out my heart as I talked to Him,

So humbled and grateful that I could come back again.

Because Someone Loved Me

I am where I'm at in my life today,

Because someone loved me, and they prayed.

And even when I could not see,

Someone who cared was praying for me.

And when I felt like I could not trust,

My name again was lifted up.

To God above who really cares,

By someone who has seen God's answered prayers.

Who knows that God is the only way?

For He makes things right in our lives today.

His love and grace, and mercy to,

Are things He shares with me and you.

Down on bended knees God hears and sees,

Every time someone who cares is praying for me.

Beauty For Ashes

Beauty for ashes how can that be,

This is something that I never thought could happen to me.

The ashes that I have carried with me all of my life,

Were a part of who I was even though it wasn't right.

Beauty for ashes who would even want to trade,

Surly no one would ever look at me in that kind of way.

There are so many others whose beauty shines bright,

Mine was covered with ashes that was dark like the night.

Beauty for ashes how can this even be true,

As tears filled my eyes I told myself this can't happen to you.

There are lots of scars and flaws that you carry around,

Still trying to find a place to put them forever down.

Beauty for ashes I heard God softly say,

Give them all to me I've been waiting for this day.

With kindness and love He took everyone,

Tossing them to the wind saying "I've just begun".

Beauty for ashes my child keep your eyes on me,

As your beauty shines through you for everyone to see.

Begin Each Day

Begin each day in faith and love,

Giving all your problems to God above.

Begin each day with hope and trust,

Knowing we have a Father who takes care of us.

Begin each day with joy and happiness,

Grateful to our Father because we're so blessed.

Begin each day with whispered prayers,

For the ones we love knowing our Father cares.

Begin each day walking in Gods ways,

Following His footsteps throughout your day.

Begin each day basking in the sun,

 Always asking God for His will to be done.

Begin each day in Gods mercy and grace,

Following His light that shines in every place.

Begin each day before your feet hit's the floor,

Expecting less but with God getting more.

Believe

Believe that the sun will shine after the rain,

And that Jesus is coming back to this world again.

Believe that the trials you have are not here to stay,

And that with God all things are possible for He'll make a way.

Believe that there is hope for all the bad things you see,

And never forget that God said "put your trust in me".

Believe when you don't understand and you ask God why?

And remember He will be the one that gives you a reason to try.

Believe when your heart is broken and you don't know what to do,

And never forget that it can be mended by your Father who created you.

Believe when you see the things that others don't always understand,

And be grateful because in your heart you know this is a part of God's plan.

Believe your life has a purpose and how special you are,

And thank God when you look back and realize you've come so far.

Believe when you look up with God dreams do come true,

And how special you are because your heavenly Father loves you.

Believe and your life will be filled with so many blessings from above,

And you will forever be grateful that you are covered by Gods love.

Blessing's In Every Step

Life's journey is full of surprises for me,

And with each step I take sometimes it's hard to see.

The mountain top that I am looking for,

The trials can be hard, I don't want them no more.

Down on my knees I go to God,

Asking is this the pathway you want me to trod?

Gently He reminds me how even Jesus wept,

And He showed me there were blessings in every step.

That I try to hurry while on my way,

Looking only for the mountain top every day.

He told me that when I finally slow down,

I would see blessings in every step I take all around.

And life's journey would mean so much more to me,

When all of His blessings I finally see

Eva Dimel | 28
Eva's Inspirations

Bridge of Dreams

I want to walk across the bridge of dreams and linger for a while,

Thinking of all the dreams I've had especially the ones that make me smile.

I want to think about the things I have and forget the dreams I lost,

Knowing that I am so blessed because of what those dreams would of cost.

I want to take my time and enjoy the view, and all the beauty I see,

On this beautiful bridge of dreams that God has created for me.

I want to just let my mind wonder as I sit here all alone,

Breathing in fresh air, looking up at the sky talking to my Father on His throne.

I want my heart to always be filled with hope every time that I come here,

Grateful for this bridge of dreams and all the things my Father shares.

I want to feel the peace in my soul that only my Father can give,

As I sit back feeling so loved because I know I'm His.

When time goes by way to fast and I know that I must leave,

I smile as I am on my way taking so many good things with me.

And I know that I will always come back I always do it seems,

To spend some time with my Father above, on His beautiful bridge of dreams.

Can I Climb Up In Your Lap

Jesus can I climb up in your lap I'm having a bad day,

I just need for you to hold me and make everything ok.

I get scared and I worry and I just want to hide,

I promise if you hold me I will try hard not to cry.

I need your loving arms around me where I know that I'll be safe,

From all of life's problems that right now I just can't face.

Jesus can I climb up in your lap it is so peaceful there,

Where you always reassure me that you love me and you care.

Right now I need to rest and I know with you I can,

As you hold me close and whisper I'll take care of you again.

While sitting in your lap I always hear the Angels sing,

Bringing comfort to my soul knowing that you'll take care of everything.

Jesus can I climb up in your lap there's no other place I'd rather be,

Than in your loving arms where you give me everything I need.

Softly I hear you whisper "my arms are open wide",

Come climb up in my lap where in my love you can abide.

Come Into His Presence

Come into His presence and let Him hold you close,

He sees your life, and He knows what you need the most.

Come into His presence He is waiting just for you,

Feel His love and grace, and see all His blessings too.

Come into His presence for He is the great I Am,

He will gladly welcome you, just take His healing hand.

Come into His presence you can take your burdens there,

And gladly He will take them for He loves you and He cares.

Come into His presence you will never want to leave,

Forever you will thank Him down on bended knees.

Come into His presence for this is where you belong,

With your Father who created you, He's been waiting for so long.

Come into His presence you don't have to wait no more

For He has everything that you've been looking for.

Come into His presence where you'll forever stay,

Walking with your Father, beside you every day.

Eva Dimel
Eva's Inspirations

Dwell on Me

There is so many things that we dwell on in life,

The trials that we have and the things that aren't right.

The worries and fears, and the things we can't see,

When God softly whispers you can always dwell on me.

Dwell on the things that I am going to do,

To make everything better for your loved ones and you.

Dwell on the blessings that I send your way,

And the prayers that I answer for you every day.

Dwell on my promises that I have always kept,

And all of the good things that you haven't received yet.

Dwell on all the love that I freely give,

To everyone no matter what kind of life that you live.

Dwell on my mercy and all of my grace,

And the sacrifice my Son made when He took your place.

Dwell on the good things and then you will see,

How much better your life is when you dwell on me.

Faith

Faith is a gift from God up above,

From it comes Gods blessings and our works of love.

Faith will stand strong when doubt pounds at our door,

It gives us the strength to keep going and not answer any more.

When life is throwing stones we let them fall at our feet,

For we have God's gift of faith and it is ours to keep.

Faith let's hope bloom in our lives every day,

Giving us so many reasons to thank God as we pray.

Faith takes us so many places that we've never been,

As it continues to grow we move farther from sin.

Faith keeps looking up and always forward to tomorrow,

Never looking back dwelling on our failures and sorrows.

Faith what a blessing that God gave us to share,

With everyone that He loves showing them that He cares.

Faith that keeps us going when we sometimes want to quit,

Showing us that with God we can always make it.

Eva Dimel
Eva's Inspirations

Father's And Son's

Two men, one young one growing old, full of anger or so it seems,

Saying things to one another, talking about what their life really means.

Remembering hurtful things and painful words, that was said down through the years,

Trying hard to talk and still be strong, while holding back their tears.

Taking time to listen and understand, for they both really do love each other,

Knowing in their hearts that God is there, working to bring them both together.

Tears start to fall, as their hearts soften, and they see things through each other's eyes,

Once angry men now filled with forgiveness, as they hold each other and cry.

Two men one young, one growing old, a father and his son,

Forever grateful to God for everything, knowing the healing has begun.

Follow The Little Children

Follow the little children and watch them play,

With no worries or fears throughout their day.

Share in their laughter enjoy the smiles on their face,

Seeing through them God's loving grace.

Take time to listen they have so much to say,

Enjoy all their stories let them take your worries away.

Reach out and touch them holding them close to you,

These are the things that God wants you to do.

Return all of their kisses seeing how much that they love,

Trusting and caring like their Father in heaven above.

Pick them up when they fall down sometimes when they play,

And bow your head and share with them every time that they pray.

Believe like they do let them teach you how to trust,

Never once have they doubted that Jesus loves them so much.

Follow the little children there is so much to see,

And you will understand why God said Let the little children come to me.

God Is Writing

The book of my life God writes every day,

With His pen of love He has so much to say.

On every page there's a blessing even in the trials too,

Letting me know I am always here for you.

Some chapters are short while others are long,

For God never dwells on the things I've done wrong.

As I look back in the book there is so much I see,

How much I have changed as He continues to mold me.

Taking me so many places that I've never been,

Showing me the things that I can do through Him.

There is so much mercy and plenty of grace,

And at the end of each chapter everything falls into place.

He's the author of my life and His story I know,

I want to follow in His steps wherever He goes.

God is writing another page in my life today,

I look up and I smile as I walk in His ways.

God It's Your name

God it's your name I cherish and I love to hear,

It's engraved in my heart for to me you're always near.

It's the first name I speak when I wake each day,

And the name that I call on to guide my way.

God it's your name that is so full of power and glory,

No matter what I'm going through you know the end of my story.

It's a name above all names that brings me to my knees,

Always giving thanks to you God who supplies all my needs.

God it's your name that brings comfort and peace to my soul,

You're so loved and so wanted by the young and the old.

God you're the light in the darkness always leading the way,

And the sun that shines on me and brightens my day.

God it's your name I cherish and I love to share,

Letting everyone know that you love them and care.

No matter where I'm at or what I'm going through,

When I hear your name God I'm so grateful I have you.

God it's your name I call on when my day is done,

Thanking you for all the blessings that you share with everyone.

God Made Something

God turned the water into wine and He made the blind to see,

But I will never forget when He took nothing and made something out of me.

All because of His love and mercy He never let me go,

He has shown me things about myself that I didn't even know.

So loved so blessed is how I feel humble in every way,

For without Him I am nothing I couldn't even make it through each day.

The storms of life that tore me down the things that I've been through,

I now can see they were stepping stones that brought me closer God to you.

So many miracles so many blessings so much that you do each day, Yet you still take time to listen to me down on my knees as I pray.

No longer do I feel so all alone and like I don't belong,

For you made something out of me and showed me I was wrong.

My life has changed in so many ways since I opened my heart to you,

With excitement and hope you have shown me there is nothing you can't do.

Down this road of life as I journey on I can't wait to see,

The plans God has for my life for I'm so blessed because He loves me.

God's Blank Check

The check was blank given to me,

With my name written on it I could clearly see.

And it was signed, yes signed by God Himself,

And there was no limit to all His wealth.

If I filled it out what would I need?

All the things in life that would help me succeed.

First I needed Jesus to come into my heart,

I knew that, that was where I needed to start.

I needed hope and faith, and love,

Things that only I could receive from God above.

I needed Gods guidance to make it through each day,

And I knew that God would show me the way.

I needed strength that I did not have,

And I wanted to be happy no longer sad.

There were choices that only I could make,

But God was there to forgive me if I made a mistake.

I wanted some joy, and to be loving, and caring,

Always ready and willing, with God's love to be sharing.

Wanted to talk with God each and every day,

Knowing that He always hears me every time that I pray.

The check was blank, I could be asking for more,

Instead I'd carry it with me, to remind me what it was for.

In the amount there was no beginning or end,

Just like Gods love, a check that only He could send.

God's Broken Shells

My broken shell's I see you there,

And I want you to know just how much I care. I know all of the places that you have been,

And I can feel the pain that you are in. I have seen everything down through your life,

Your struggles and fear, and your sorrows and strife.

I watch over you all of the time,

Because I love you, and you are mine.

I know that broken is something you don't want to be,

But because you are broken there is so much that you see.

Things that others would never truly understand,

That's why I chose you to be a part of my plan.

Your compassion and love, and your caring for others,

Keeps you reaching out to your sisters and brothers.

There are so many things that broken shells can do,

For I hold the broken pieces that came from you.

With my loving hands I will put them back together,

So everyone will see a beautiful shell forever.

My broken shell's, so full of all the good things,

That touches your Father's heart,

With all the joy that you bring.

God's Love

God's love fills our hearts and fills our homes,

What a blessing with Him we are never alone.

God's love is our light on the darkest day,

Showing us that with Him we will be ok.

God's love is the Son that shines down on us,

Reminding us that in Him we can always trust.

Eva Dimel
Eva's Inspirations

God's Quilt of Love

God's quilt of love that covers me,

Has so much beauty that I can see.

The colors are all so beautiful,

There is something special that they all hold.

It comforts me when I am sad,

Gives me the hope I never had.

It touches my heart in so many ways,

God's quilt of love covers me every day.

Under God's quilt I get through so many things,

The good and the bad that this life brings.

There is so much beauty that I now can see,

Since I have God's quilt that covers me.

I found peace and joy and laughter there,

And a place to rest and leave all my cares.

Everything that I have been searching for, I now have found I need search no more.

The love, the peace, the blessings God shares,

Under God's quilt you'll find them all there.

Miracles that happen for all to see,

Because of God's love I now believe.

Under God's quilt of love that covers me today, Because of Jesus I can forever stay.

God's Return Policy

Like the prodigal son who went his own way,

God waits for you to return to Him every day.

With sadness as He watches you try on your own,

Knowing the life that He gave you wasn't meant to live alone.

After falling down you wonder can I even return.

To my Father who I need, and for whose love I yearn.

You ask yourself will He even let me come home.

There is so much I've done and so many places I've roamed.

As you make your way back you can hardly believe,

There is no line to wait in His arms are open for me.

No questions were asked and you wasn't turned away,

You didn't have to show no I D God knew you in every way.

God's return policy is filled with unconditional love,

His door is always open as He greets you with a hug.

Happy His child has returned and is finally home,

Hanging onto His hand with Him you're never alone.

Eva Dimel
Eva's Inspirations

He Came After Me

Little lost lamb afraid and alone,

Wondering so far away from home.

Not knowing which way to turn or to go,

Needing the Shepherd for He surely knows.

Hungry and tired really needing fed,

From God's precious word, where so many good things are said.

Forever a stray they do not want to be,

Suddenly they hear His voice, the Shepherd's coming after me.

Calling out their name, the Shepherd's found them, God loves all of His sheep, for they belong to Him.

What a blessing to know that at times when we stray, God will come after us, and help us find our way.

Eva Dimel
Eva's Inspirations

He Clothed Me

The line was so long but I made it at last,

Wondering what I would be wearing as I looked back at my past.

The garments of my life were all tattered and torn,

What did God see in me with the things I had worn.

I had nothing to offer but my heart and my love,

And broken pieces to my Father in heaven above.

When I came into His presence I fell to my knees,

Asking for His forgiveness would He save me please?

I felt His arms around me and a peace I'd never known,

As I heard Him whisper, I love you and you are my own.

Forgiven is what you are and you never have to look back,

My Son took on all your sins and I've forgotten your past.

I cried God I'm not worthy of all you've done for me,

And He answered I'm the only one who knows what you can be.

He clothed me in garments that was fit for a king,

His child who He loved that didn't deserve anything.

He Just Gave Up

He just gave up he lost his will,

Not knowing that God loved him still.

Life seem to hard so he just quit,

Forgetting with God that he could make it.

He packed his things and got ready to leave,

With tears in his eyes he could hardly see.

Feeling all alone he closed the door,

Never wanting to look back any more.

Slowly he began to walk away,

When a loving voice called his name that day.

I'm here for you and I love you so,

Sit down let's talk before you go.

I know that you don't understand,

But for your life I have a plan.

Open your heart and let me in,

You'll never feel alone again.

Your life will change and you'll be set free,

For you will now be walking with me.

He felt the Son shine all around,

And where real love was truly found.

He just gave up the things he did not need,

To his Father who loved him and helped him see.

He Never Met A Stranger

He never met a stranger, for everyone He knew, their first, their last, their middle names,

He knew their whole life to. He never turned anyone away, no matter what they had done,

Coming to Him was the only way, for He was God's only Son.

He never said an unkind word the truth was all He spoke, Telling us all how to live our lives, knowing He was our only hope.

He went to places others would not go because He really cared,

He never worried about what others thought, He had a message to share.

He taught the fishermen how to fish, in more than just one way,

For He knew everything that they would need, to survive in life one day.

He told of things that was to come, so everyone would know,

And He promised if they followed Him, someday with Him they'd go.

He never judged or said harsh things, when some turned their backs on Him,

For He understood and no matter what, in His heart He still loved them.

He healed the blind, and helped the lame to walk, He touched every life He'd see,

And He has never stopped, even today, He still takes care of you and me.

Heavenly Eyes

Heavenly eyes are watching over me,

Seeing the things that I cannot see.

Watching the steps that I take every day,

Guiding my way when I start to stray.

Heavenly eyes that are full of love,

Belonging to my Father, God above.

Never forgetting me no matter what,

Helping me through life, with His healing touch.

Heavenly eyes that sees me when I cry,

Reaching down, He wipes the tears from my eyes.

Knowing how much that I need Him,

He answers my prayers time and again.

Heavenly eyes that knows everything,

With love in His heart, to me His comfort He brings.

Helping me every day He holds onto my hand,

Showing me that through Him, my life has a plan.

Heavenly eyes that sees all of my sins,

Forgiving me because I belong to Him,

Showing me compassion, and molding my life,

Giving me peace in my heart for I'm never out of His site.

Heavenly eyes watching over me as I sleep,

So true to His word, all His promises He keeps.

Heaven's Over Flowing

Oh what a blessing it is everywhere I go,

Heaven's overflowing with Gods love for us I know.

It's overflowing into houses that have never been a home,

And it's touching so many lives who now no longer feel alone.

It's in the streets it's on the highways and the cars are slowing down,

No one wants to miss a minute heaven's over flowing it's all around.

All of Gods children are standing still, looking up so filled with Awe,

Wondering if this is the moment they will hear their Fathers call.

Broken lives are being mended and the weak they now are strong,

Heaven's over flowing with the bread of life that we need to carry on.

There's a calmness everywhere as Gods peace and love we see,

Heaven is over flowing touching everyone including me.

People are reaching out with love that they have never felt before,

All because heaven is over flowing God with His love opened the door.

I Expect To Much

I expect to much God in so many ways,

I want my life to be perfect in every way.

I want everyone to be happy with the things that they have,

No more sickness or pain and no reason to be sad.

I want sunshine every day and clouds that are blue,

And I want to always love everything in life that I do.

I want everyone to get along and all the wars to end,

And I want this world to forever be free from all sin.

I want no more children going hungry and feeling unloved,

And I want every dream to come true while looking above.

I want everyone to know just how special they are,

To the one who created the moon and the stars.

I expect way to much God please forgive me today,

As I hear you softly whisper my child you're thinking my way.

I Found

I found God's Heavenly grace,

In this earthly place.

When I needed it so much,

I found God's healing touch.

When there was no hope to be found,

I realized God was around.

When all I could do was cry,

I felt God's comfort by my side.

When I was so full of fear,

I heard God whisper I am here.

When I worried throughout the day,

God showed me He'd make a way.

When I felt I could not trust,

God helped me realize, in Him I must.

When I questioned could I go on?

Filled my heart with a beautiful song.

When I worried about growing old,

Gods loving peace filled my soul.

When there were things I did not understand,

God reassured me, it was a part of His plan.

When I thought everything was lost,

God showed me His Son Jesus, paid the cost.

I Have So Much To Be Thankful For

Dear God I have so much to be thankful for,

I could live the rest of my life and never ask for more.

Your love, and your mercy, and all of your grace,

The closeness I feel with you, nothing could ever take your place.

Looking down through my life and where I now am,

Gives me peace in my heart for it was with you I began.

The everyday blessings no matter how small,

Mean so much to me, I am grateful for them all.

The way that you listen every day when I pray,

Caring so much about everything that I have to say.

My family and friends, and my loved ones who care,

The way you let me know that for me you're always there.

And the times when I need you to help me the most,

You wipe my tears and you comfort me and hold me so close.

You're my strength when I'm weak, and my hope when I'm stressed,

You're my answer to life's problems, with you I'm so blessed.

My love for you grows even stronger with each passing day,

I have so much to be thankful for because of you in every way.

I Looked Up

I looked down and I found that everything looked bad,

I looked back and I saw so many things that were sad.

I looked up and I could feel the sun shine on my face,

I felt love, and I felt peace, and Gods Heavenly grace.

I realized everyday what I needed to do,

No matter what I was doing, or what I was going through.

If I looked down I missed the hope, and the strength for the day,

If I looked back I'd dwell on things, I could not change anyway.

But looking up I would find everything that I need,

 I'd have a reason to keep trying, knowing with God I could succeed.

Every day as I pray I ask God for His will,

Knowing He takes care of me, and no matter what He loves me still.

And when I'm down, and feeling like there is no hope around,

I look up and I realize, where true hope is found.

When I look back and I worry about, what has already been done?

I look up and I see the battles over, and my Father has won.

Yes looking up my soul is filled, with Gods peace, and Gods love,

My life is blessed every day, because of my Father above.

I Wait and I Watch

I wait and I watch for my heavenly Father who's always there,

To embrace me and help me for He truly cares.

I wait and I watch filled with hope from above,

For the one who created me out of His love.

I wait and I watch knowing He will answer me,

When I call on His name I can feel the victory.

Over the trials and the problems in everyday life,

The sadness and sorrows He makes everything all right.

Even the small things I gladly give them all to Him,

If it bothers me He will answer my prayers again.

I wait and I watch and there's so much that I see,

With peace in my heart, for my Fathers on His way to help me.

I Wish For You

I wish for you enough sun to shine on you every day,

But to never forget the trials that you've had along the way.

I wish for you enough happiness to make your spirit soar,

But to never forget what you're smiling for.

I wish for you enough pain so that you can see,

That God is always there for you and for me.

I wish for you enough loss so that you can appreciate,

Everything that you have and that it was worth the wait.

I wish for you enough compassion, and love to share,

With someone who needs to know that somebody cares.

I wish for you everything that God wants you to have,

Never forgetting to thank Him through the good and the bad.

I wish for you all the things in life that you will need,

Knowing that the most important ones are from God, and they're free.

I Worry

I worry and I fret through most of my day,

Never taking the time to just stop and pray.

I think about everything that could possibly go wrong,

When in my heart I could be praising God all day long.

I get tired and I'm stressed and I don't even smile,

I've got too much on my mind when I could stop for a while.

I want to enjoy this life that God gave to me,

With tears in my eyes I ask God for His help please.

In my heart He answers quit looking ahead,

You know that with me you have nothing to dread.

Look up when you worry for I'm here for you,

And there is so many things that I want you to do.

Things that will keep you busy and make you happy,

You just need to pack up your worries and give them to me.

I worry and I fret not as much anymore,

I'm to busy doing things for my precious Lord

I'll Never See The End

I'll never see the end of the ocean or the bright blue sea,

Or the stars in the sky and the sun that shines down on me.

I'll never see the end of my loved ones their lives will go on,

In the heavens above so grateful to God they belong.

I'll never see the end of a rainbow it has no beginning or end,

Another promise from God to never flood this world again.

I'll never see the end of Gods miracles He performs every day,

Touching and blessing His children in so many ways.

I'll never see the end of people praying to their Father above,

Who listens and answers in His time with love.

I'll never see the end of hope that we need every day,

For with God all things are possible He will show us the way.

I'll never see the end of Gods mercy, His love and His grace,

As I wake each morning knowing nothing could ever take His place.

I'M BUILDING MY HOME

I don't have much Lord but I'm starting today,

And I'm going to need your help in every way I'm building my home on your promises, and love,

Could you please send me the materials I need from above?

I know I have tried to build my home many times,

With all the wrong things Lord leaving what I needed behind.

And every time it fell I would try again,

Feeling hopeless and wondering where do I even begin?

Today I feel so blessed because I am starting with you,

Knowing that you will show me what I need to do.

This time my home after the storms will still stand,

For it will be built on solid rock instead of sinking sand.

No more will I have to worry or be afraid it will fall,

Because I will always have you, and on your name I can call.

My home will have comfort and peace I've never known,

Things I never had when I tried to build it alone.

It will be filled with so much love, and faith, and trust,

Lord I'm so excited I've never had a home built by us.

I'm building my home with a brand new plan,

Every part of it will be finished by the Masters strong hand.

I'm Cleaning Out My Heart

I'm cleaning out my heart it has been a long time,

I'm getting rid of all the trash and the junk that I find.

I know there is a lot of things that I've stored there for years,

Lots of sorrows and bad things like worries and fears.

I'm starting today and I'm finally ready to look inside,

I know it will take a while I could not do it in a day if I tried.

I just want to rush right through it and not feel anything that is there.

I'm afraid that I might cry when I see the times I thought no one cared.

When I finally looked inside my heart I could not believe what I saw,

As my eyes filled with tears I was so blessed and in Awe.

Jesus was there with His light shining so bright,

All the bad things were gone and my heart was alright.

He smiled at me and I could feel His love all over again,

As He softly said I cleaned your heart, when you asked me in.

I'm Going To Smile

I'm going to smile at someone every day,

And keep the faith no matter what comes my way.

I'm going to share all the happiness that God gives,

Showing someone that they have a reason to live.

I'm going to share everything that I have,

With someone else who's in need and is sad.

I'm going to reach out and give someone a hug,

Letting them know just how much they are loved.

I'm going to take time just to listen to someone,

Thanking God for everything that He's done.

I'm going to take the time to enjoy all the blessings I see,

Forever grateful that God is using me.

Yes I'm going to reach out and go that extra mile,

And because of God I am going to smile.

I'm Growing In His Love

I'm growing in His love a little more each day,

I noticed we get closer every time I pray.

He showers me with kindness His mercy and His grace,

I'm growing in His love it's all over the place.

No matter where I go or what I'm going through,

His love is always there whispering I'll take care of you.

I'm growing in His love so much that I now share,

So many things He's given me letting everyone know I care.

I feel so good inside and my heart it over flows,

So wanted and so loved God always lets me know.

I'm growing in His love as He tends to all my needs,

Just like a lovely flower that started as a seed.

I'm blooming where I'm at in so many ways,

He touched my life, and I'm so blessed growing in every way.

I'm Home

The road I traveled was so very long,

But it was one that I knew I had to stay on.

There was mountains and valleys and times that were rough,

But I hung in there I never wanted to give up.

I fought with every ounce of strength that I had,

Hanging onto Gods hand when times get too bad.

I had so much that I wanted to live for,

My family and my loved ones and so much more.

The time finally came and now my fighting's done,

I'm at peace with my Father the saving one.

What a blessing it was when I stepped in the door,

Heavens everything I dreamed of and even more.

I have laughed so much with my family and friends,

Walked on streets of gold my joy never ends.

There is nothing but beauty everywhere,

Blue skies and sunshine and my Father who cares.

We sat in the garden and talked for hours,

While the birds softly sang enjoying the beautiful flowers.

I thanked Him and praised Him as tears filled my eyes,

He held me close as He whispered in heaven no one cries.

I smiled knowing all of His promises were true,

How could anyone be sad God while living with you?

I know your hearts are heavy and you're feeling alone,

Instead of crying please thank God, I've made it, I'm home.

I'm Leaning

I'm leaning on the cross today,

And trusting God to guide my way.

Through the storms and the trials that are in my life,

Knowing He can take everything and make it alright.

I'm leaning when I feel like I can't stand,

As I hold on to God's strong and steady hand.

Grateful that for me he is always there,

The one who loves me and truly cares.

I'm leaning as the tears start to flow,

While He holds me close and lets me know.

That I never have to leave His side,

In His comfort and love I can always abide.

I'm leaning and so blessed that I always can,

On my heavenly Father who created who I am.

I'm Learning How To Fly

I'm spreading my wings as I learn how to fly,

For me all things are possible with God by my side.

I'm doing new things that I thought couldn't be done,

Laughing and trying while on this journey having fun.

I'm walking not running taking one step at a time,

Stopping to smell the roses knowing with God I'll be fine.

I'm climbing new mountains that I said I never will,

Making it to the top watching God turn it to a hill.

I'm taking chances and learning how to let go,

Of the things in my life that God will take care of I know.

I'm looking up and letting the sun shine down on me,

So grateful to God for all the beauty and blessings I see.

Yes I'm spreading my wings and I'm learning to fly,

It's time in my life God has opened my eyes.

I'm Leaving Behind

No matter where I go today,

I'm leaving some things behind as I go on my way.

Something's that I just want to share,

Letting everyone know just how much I care.

Because of my Father who has shown me how,

To share His gifts with everyone now.

I'll be leaving some love so that everyone knows,

How much that they mean where ever I go.

I have plenty of hugs that I'm sharing to,

Letting God's love show through me to you.

Kindness and compassion I have plenty to give,

Forever grateful to God for showing me how to live.

A shoulder to cry on and God's strength to get by,

Reminding everyone that God never leaves their side.

Happiness and joy, I'm leaving that behind to,

God has given me so much, to share with you.

Yes I'll be leaving behind so many things today,

Thanking God for His blessings, as He shows me the way.

I'm Resting

There is so much to do and so much to face,

I'm resting today in God's heavenly grace.

Away from life's troubles and all of life's trials,

I'm resting in my Fathers love for a little while.

Forgetting all my troubles and all of my cares,

Knowing with God I can leave them all there.

No running around no answering phones,

I'm resting and spending time with my Father alone.

He quietly listens as I talk to Him,

Letting go of my fears, I realize I'm resting again.

Just basking in His love that comforts me,

Knowing that I am where I need to be.

Enjoying letting go and the peace that I feel,

Grateful to have a Father who takes care of me still.

What a wonderful place that I'm so happy to be,

As my Father softly whispers "when you need rest come to me".

In everyone's heart

In everyone's heart there is a prayer,

Needing to know someone loves them and cares.

Wanting to feel the touch of Gods hand,

Feeling empty inside needing a plan.

While crying out in so many ways,

Still holding back not wanting to pray.

With so many things they don't want to let go,

As they hear the words Jesus loves me I know.

They are afraid to step out on faith alone,

Taking so many chances as they move farther from home.

The storms of life come and they try to hang on,

As everything seems to be going wrong.

They hear the words trust, forgiveness and grace,

These are the things that will get you out of this place.

The things only your heavenly Father can give to you,

And there's only one thing you have to do.

It's been in your heart waiting for you to say,

My child it is time come to me and pray.

Into Gods Hands

Into Gods hands I place all of my treasures,

Knowing that he will take care of them forever.

All of my children my family and friends,

The list goes on it never does end.

Life's problems and sorrows, I place them all there,

Thankful to God for how much He loves me and cares.

Trusting, from my hands I gladly give,

Into Gods hands all the things that are His.

With love in my heart and peace in my soul,

I now can be happy for the things I no longer hold.

Into Gods hands I have placed everything,

While watching Him work I see all the blessings He brings.

Letting go is not easy but God showed me I can,

For the things that I carry are to big for my hands.

Into Gods hands I humbly put mine,

Knowing that with Him, in my life I'll be fine.

It's Going to Take a Miracle

So many times I have heard these words said,

From the ones that I love as they were filled with dread.

There is nothing we can do there is no hope to be found,

When I see so many blessings for our Father's always around.

With tears in their eyes and hearts broken in two,

I hear it's going to take a miracle, what are we going to do.

My heart fills with compassion and plenty of love,

For I know that all miracles comes from our Father above

.Down on my knees with my head bowed in prayer,

I hear my Father whisper I'm on my way I'll be right there.

He is the answer to every prayer that I pray,

The miracle worker and He's on His way.

He knows every need and He sees every tear,

All the suffering and pain and for us He's always here.

He's touched so many lives with His healing hands,

My heavenly Father how I love Him, the great I am.

When I hear it's going to take a miracle, with hope I can say,

I'll talk to the miracle worker down on my knees as I pray.

It's Time

It's time to be happy and let go of the past,

Time to slow down, for life goes to fast.

It's time to rejoice and thank God above,

For all of His blessings and all of His love.

It's time to forgive and set your mind free,

Making more room for all the good things you see.

It's time to start sharing, expecting nothing in return,

Something our Heavenly Father taught us, it's time to learn.

It's time to stop and smell the flowers each day,

And to take their fragrance with us as we go on our way.

It's time to love more unconditionally,

Something that God does for you and for me.

It's time to let go of all your worries and fears,

We don't have to carry them for God is right here.

It's time to do nothing some days and relax,

Refreshing your soul knowing it's ok to sit back.

It's time, and God gave it to each one of us,

To use as we chose because He loves us so much.

It's time a precious gift to always be thankful for,

For there are some who have little and wish they had more.

I've Had

I've had heartaches and sorrow, and days filled with pain,

I've had blue skies and sunshine, and no reason to complain.

I've had many tears that have fallen, and many times that I've cried,

I've had laughter and fun, and success when I tried.

I've had worry, fear and doubt, that would not go away,

I've had peace joy and comfort, and strength for the day.

I've had disappointment and wondered why things happened to me,

I've had someone to love, how much happier could I be?

I've had things I had to go through, that I wouldn't wish on anyone,

I've had forgiveness from my Father, who sacrificed for me His only Son.

I have someone who walks beside me, and holds onto my hand,

I have someone who loves me unconditionally, just as I am.

I have a future to look forward to, that only my heavenly Father can see,

I have everything because my Father knows, just what I need.

Eva Dimel
Eva's Inspirations

I've Learned In Life

As life goes on down through the years,

I've learned that there will be heartaches and sometimes tears.

I've lost things that I've loved and wondered why,

I've learned that it's ok to break down and cry.

I have done things looking back now that I regret,

But I learned that I've been forgiven, and God's not done with me yet.

There were so many changes that life threw at me,

And I learned that it was God showing me, how much more I could be

I've had my share of failures, and success along life's way, I learned these brought me closer to God as I prayed.

I remember thinking I needed to have everything,

And I have learned that true happiness only God can bring.

I thought that I knew all I needed to know,

But I learned I needed Gods love through me to show.

As life goes on I pray that I always see,

The good things in life that God is still teaching me.

Just For Today

Just for today I will let my worries be,

And just think about the things that makes me happy.

I won't dwell on the problems from yesterday or tomorrow,

I'm giving them to God I don't need all that sorrow.

Just for today I am going to relax in the sun,

And enjoy all the beauty thanking God for all He's done.

I have been through some storms but my lifeguard was there,

Bringing me through everyone for He loves me and cares.

Just for today I'm going to laugh more and love,

And remember all my blessings God sent me from above.

There were times in my life when I could not even smile,

But they soon were gone they only lasted a little while.

Just for today I'm going to enjoy my family and friends,

As I realize with God just how blessed that I am.

I've had anger and been hurt, and things that I wouldn't let go,

Then God taught me how to forgive there's so much that He knows.

Just for today I have so many good things to do,

All because of my heavenly Father, God I'm so grateful to you.

Just One More Time Lord

Dear Lord my heart is breaking in two right now,

Could you please send my loved one back for a little while?

I just need to hug them one more time,

I promise after I do I will be fine.

I know that I'll stop crying and I won't shed no more tears,

Just for a little while Lord, I really need them here.

"My child I love you so much" and there's nothing for you,

I would not do.

But your loved one is so happy I'm taking good care of them too.

I know that you are sad right now and missing them so much,

It was time for them to come home they really needed their Fathers touch.

I know that you don't understand and on earth you never will,

And even though you're so very sad your loved one is with you still.

In every memory you have, and inside your heart each day,

I promise you it will get better and the pain will go away.

There will still be times you shed a tear when you are thinking of them,

But with love you know because of me you will be with them once again.

Just one more time Lord I really wish that this Prayer would come true,

But in my heart I have so much peace because I know that they're with you.

Land Of The Free

Land of the free home of the brave,

Pray for the ones who are fighting for us every day.

Families torn apart loved ones that are missed,

I pray we never ever forget this.

God's on our side He has everything we need,

Thank God we are so blessed to live in the land of the free.

Letter From God

If you believe in the bible and Me and the cross,

While you're following man who is leading the lost.

Ignoring what I said when you know what is true,

All because you want laws now to be ok with what you do.

Man's laws are not mine and they never will be,

You can't have it both ways if you're following me.

It's been thousands of years and My word has not changed,

The bible was not written for anyone to rearrange.

It's not man that you call on when you need help from above,

I'm the one who created you out of My love.

You have seen what I can do if you've followed Me,

Your Forefathers went by my word in this land of the free.

It breaks My heart seeing what so many have done,

But in the end you will see My way is the only one.

You can say that you love Me no matter how you chose to live,

I am God who sees everything, even the things that you've hid.

One day you will need Me and it could be soon,

If you read My word then you know this world is domed.

I'll be coming back to this world one day,

Taking all of My children who have followed My ways.

I hope you'll be one of them; remember you get to choose,

You are My child who I love, with so much to lose.

Letter From Heaven

If I could write a letter and send it down to you,

There's so much I would tell you, there's so much here to do.

There are angels on every corner, the beauty is so grand,

When I first arrived here, God Himself He took my hand.

I've met all of my family, they're so loving and so kind,

I gave them all an update on everyone they've left behind.

Their smiles are never ending, they tell me their happiness never ends,

For here in heaven, there is no heartache, for It's not been touched by sin.

My first thought was for my family and my loved ones I hold so dear,

There were so many things I would have said knowing my homecoming was so near.

I Would have told you how much I loved you, and thanked you for all that you've done for me,

All of you are the very best, God gave me such a loving family.

I know this is very hard on you and your tears seem never ending,

That's why I asked God to please allow me to send this letter I'm sending.

Heaven is so very beautiful, I've walked on streets of gold,

There is no sickness here or pain, and no one ever grows old.

All the fields here are filled with flowers, there is greenery everywhere,

There's so much love, laughter and fun, and our Father who really cares.

I talked to God about you and poured my love out to Him,

He put His arms around me, and reassured me we'd be together again.

For now He sends His strength and love, and He'll carry you if need be,

I want you to know He's such a loving God, I know someday you will see.

I want you all to please be strong and carry me close to your heart,

You have the rest of your lives to live, my prayer is that you will start.

The joy you gave me through the years, I want that joy for you,

Take time to live, to love, to laugh and through you, let me shine through.

And when you think of me, don't think of me with tears, think of me with laughter,

For God has given me a home, where I'll live happily ever after.

Light Of My Life

Light of my life love of my heart,

I pray God from you I never do part.

Hope for my day, peace in my soul,

God it is your hand that I always hold.

Grace for each day, love that is true,

These are the things God I get from you.

Light of my life that guides me every day,

Showing me I can trust for you are the way.

The truth that helps me to understand,

All things are possible with your unchanging plans.

Door's that are opened that once were closed,

In my heart thanking you for it's your blessings I know.

Light of my life the one I'm so grateful for,

As long as I have you God I will never need more.

Look To Me

Look to me for your hope,

When you feel you can't cope.

And life's problems seem never ending,

Call out my name and I'll be there,

I'll help you with all your cares,

Look around and you'll see all the blessings I'm sending.

Each and everyday things will change,

For nothing ever remains the same.

And you'll realize your life is getting better,

I'll be there to see you through,

For I'll never stop watching over you.

I'm God your Father and I'll love you forever.

Take time to laugh when you want to cry,

Knowing that this trial will soon pass by.

And that your strength will always come from me.

Give your problems to me just let them go,

My love and grace is sufficient you know.

Never forget you are a child of the King.

Lord Will You Please Check On Me

Dear Lord, I'm trying very hard to live my life the right way,

I need you Lord if you don't mind to please check on me throughout my day.

I know that I will stumble, and at times I will even fall,

But I know that you'll be there for me to help me through it all.

I want to live my life for you for all the world to see,

And I need your love, and guidance, and for you to please check on me.

There are times I know that I get scared no matter how hard I try,

And at times I feel defeated and I just want to cry.

Its times like this I need you so much, so I'll ask you once again,

Lord will you please check on me, I'm facing a battle that I need you to win.

I want to spread your joy, and love, and hope with everyone I see,

And I want to brag on you, and how blessed I am, because your only Son, was crucified for me.

There is so many things that I want to do, and I pray that I won't fail

I need you Lord to please check on me and make sure everything is going well.

And when night time comes, and I am tired with nothing else to do,

I want to always praise your holy name, and never ever forget to thank you.

And when I close my eyes and I fall asleep with sweet memories on my mind,

Lord I pray that you will check on me through the night just one more time.

Lost Love

Lost love broken hearts will they ever mend?

In life we are blessed to have a chance to love again.

Someone new, someone different in so many ways,

When we least expect it comes into our life one day.

Learning to trust and to care as we let go of the past,

Willing to try again not worrying how long it will last.

Sharing yourself with someone knowing there's so much to do,

Lost love broken hearts in life love always comes back to you.

Loving Jesus

Loving Jesus more and more every day,

Forever grateful that He shows me the way.

To the Master God's Heavenly home,

Where I know I will never again be alone.

Loving Jesus for all that He has done,

Sacrificing His life so that we could have one.

Taking on each and everyone's sins,

Loving us so much He would do it all again.

Loving Jesus who teaches us how to live,

Walking in His love He shows us how to give.

Knowing we can be happy and so filled with love,

Forever grateful to God up above.

Loving Jesus, He is my everything,

Showing me all the good to my life that He brings.

Making my life complete in every way,

Yes loving Jesus who is with me every day.

Memory Lane

Let's take a walk down memory lane,

To places we know we'll never go again.

I want to see all the good times, and the ones I love to,

And I want to reminisce about the things that I use to do.

Let's stay for a while at the places we love,

And give thanks for those times to our Father above.

Let's spend time with the ones who are no longer here,

The ones whose memories we hold so dear.

I want to linger at the places that I use to call home,

Where I had no worries, or fears of my own.

Where Mom and Dad took care of everything,

And I could be a child, oblivious to what life could bring.

I want to stop and smell the flowers along the way,

Knowing my Father watches over me every day.

And when it's time to come back to where I now am,

I want to thank God for all the wonderful places I have been.

My Baggage

The train pulled up I could not wait I really wanted to leave,

I had a ticket that I clung to it was freely given to me.

All of those years that I spent searching for happiness and peace,

Not knowing that someone loved me so much they died so I could be free.

So many had tried to tell me but I didn't seem to care,

Everything that I thought I needed could be found in my world here.

I did what I wanted thinking I'm ok I know just what I need,

But the people who loved me were praying and slowly planting seeds.

My world came crashing down on me and I didn't know where to turn,

And then I remembered all those prayers and thank God I finally learned.

Down on my knees I cried to God and He gently wiped my tears,

Reassuring me that I would be ok because He would always be here.

I now was ready to take that train God had saved a seat for me,

There was so much love and comfort there, and so much God wanted me to see.

I climbed on board carrying all my baggage ready to start this new life of mine,

When the conductor came up and whispered to me, you'll be leaving all that baggage behind.

As I let it go it felt so good I finally could be free,

With peace in my soul and love in my heart I knew God was all I'd ever need.

My Brothers Shoes

My brother's shoes looked so good to me,

I wanted to wear them would they fit let me see.

There were so many different kinds,

From all walks of life but none like mine.

They had to be better than the ones I wore,

Their lives seemed perfect and I needed them more.

I found a pair and slipped them on,

They felt so good how could I go wrong.

I started to walk in my brothers shoes,

Seeing so many things that I never knew.

How much he struggled every day,

And the things in life that got in his way.

The burdens that he carried feeling all alone,

Never knowing where these shoes would someday roam.

With tears in my eyes I felt his pain,

I never wanted to wear his shoes again.

Down on my knees I went to God in prayer,

Asking Him to keep my brother in His loving care.

To hold his hand and to guide his way,

And to stay by his side every day.

As I took his shoes off and put mine back on,

I thanked God up above I was where I belonged.

My Child

My child I want to talk to you today,

There is so many things that I want to say.

But most importantly I need you to know,

That my love is with you no matter where you go.

I watch over you every day,

And I know your life and I see your ways.

I know when you are hurt and you cry,

There is nothing about you that passes me by.

I see your struggles and how you fear,

Please trust me and know that I am always near.

I know you worry about a lot of things,

Never forget that I am here no matter what life brings

In sickness and pain, and bad times too,

I am there and never will I ever leave you

I love it when I see you smile,

And you forget all your troubles in life for a while.

I love your laughter and the joy you share,

Knowing you have a Father who loves you and cares.

I love it when you talk to me,

Knowing I have the answer for all life's problems you see.

I love showering you with blessings, and my grace from above,

But most of all my child, I want you to know that your loved.

Not just in the good times, but the bad times too

Every day every moment, I will forever love you.

My Future

I don't know about my future and my past is already gone,

But I'm living today and trusting with God I'm right where I belong.

Sometimes I start to worry then I'm reminded my future's in His hands,

Then my worry turns to excitement as I wonder what He has planned.

I'm so grateful He walks before me always taking the time to make a way,

My heavenly Father who's always with me at the beginning and end of my day.

It's His love that keeps me going and gives me so many reasons to try,

With Him I'm never thirsty He's the living well that never runs dry.

He has everything I need in my life and He loves it when I come to Him,

Humbly on bended knees praying and asking for what I need again.

As I walk this path before me I know with God I will never be alone,

For I feel His presence with me and I'm so thankful for me He left His throne.

With Him I'm free to dream my dreams and believe in all the good I see,

Even in the bad times I know He is there and He truly does love me.

I don't know about my future but I have a loving Father who knows everything,

And with peace in my heart I no longer worry about what my future will bring.

My God, My Father

Through the darkness, and through the pain,

My God, My Father, stills gives me a reason to sing.

Through the trials of everyday life,

He gives me the strength that I need to fight.

My God, My Father, who loves me so,

Takes hold of my hand showing me which way to go.

And when I feel like all hope is gone,

My God, My Father, shows me I can carry on.

And when I go for days, and see no sunshine,

My God, My Father, on me lets His light shine.

No matter what happens my life is in His hands,

My God, My Father, who loves me and understands.

My Heart Gets In The Way

As a mother it's so hard to make the best decisions every day,

Even though God has shown me my heart still gets in the way.

I hear Him whisper if you don't let go, how can I do anything,

You protect your child from all the consequences that their choices bring.

Do you think that you are helping do they love you any more,

They still do what they want to as they walk in and out of your door.

I have shown you what they love now and what they'll continue to do,

It breaks my heart to see you crying you forgot you're important too.

You have raised them sacrificing giving them everything they need,

They are grown now let them go so that they will come to me.

As a mother you are loving and I know you really care,

But your standing in the way for their true help starts right here.

My arms are open I've been waiting for I also love them too,

I want you to enjoy your life but I see them destroying you.

They have problems and they need help but not the kind that you can give

All things are possible I will show you give them the chance to live.

I know it's painful and it hurts just lean on me I'm always here,

I will help you as you let go and release them to my care

My Mothers Prayers

I miss my mother's loving prayers,

I took for granted she'd always be here.

I always called her and together we'd pray,

For whoever needed Gods touch that day?

There was so many times she would pray for me,

Her faith was so strong and she always believed.

And when God answered she would praise His name,

Always so grateful that He answered her prayers again.

Looking up towards heaven I asked God to help me please,

I miss my mother's prayers that always comforted me.

"My child "He whispered your mother prays all the time,

And she knows how much I love you and that you will be fine.

She walks with me and we talk every day,

And I listen with love to everything she has to say.

My Resignation

I'm turning in my resignation

I'm giving it to God today,

The job I've found is too big

I've tried to do everything my way.

I thought that I was qualified to help change my problems and life,

And now I've really messed things up trying to make everything all right.

I would always go to God in prayer and give Him everything,

Not realizing I was still hanging on doubting, can I really trust Him?

I thought I could really help God, with just a little advice,

I knew how I wanted things to be I didn't even have to think twice.

But God with all His wisdom and mercy and grace,

Knows everything in life I need and the trials I'm going to face.

I'm turning in my resignation and letting God take care of things,

I don't need the heartbreak and sorrow that hanging onto life's problems brings.

My Savior's Throne Room

I saw the room and entered in,

Not knowing what to say or where to begin.

I've seen the throne, no turning back now,

I just wanted to stay there for a while.

With my head bowed down and shaking knees,

I couldn't see Him but I knew He'd seen me.

Suddenly the room was all aglow,

I could feel His presence, I never wanted to go.

The love, the peace, the grace was there,

As I found my way over to His chair.

With my head bowed down, I got on my knees,

Forever grateful to Him for making time for me.

And like a child I begin to cry,

He reached out to me. He never passed me by.

With loving arms, He held me close,

My God, my Father, the one I loved the most.

I poured out my heart, I was weary and tired,

He comforted me, He knew life could be hard.

He reached out and wiped my tears away,

Telling me when times get hard, He would make a way.

As I stood to go, He took my hand,

And told me I was always welcome to come back again.

My Saviors throne room always open for me,

A place to leave my burdens and be set free.

My Tour Guide

God didn't hand me a ticket like a travel agent would do,

He said I will be your tour guide on this journey of life with you.

You will never be alone for I will always be your guide,

Holding onto your hand staying right by your side.

I will protect you and walk with you through the storms in your life,

For my love and my mercy will make everything alright.

There is so many things in life that I want you to see,

Through the eyes of your Father as you journey on with me.

Every trial has a reason and every life a story to tell,

As your tour guide I've been through it and I know it all so well.

All the things that you feel and everything that you go through,

Are things that Jesus went through on His journey to save you?

Who better than someone who's been there and truly understands,

Everything that you'll be needing to live the life that God has planned.

With so much love God gives me so many reason to keep going every day,

He's my tour guide what a blessing who I love in every way.

On This Side of Heaven

On this side of heaven there is so much that I see,

That makes me grateful for my Savior who truly loves me.

There is heartache and suffering and sometimes lots of tears,

But my heavenly Father has promised I won't always live here.

On this side of heaven God teaches me more every day,

Just how happy I can be when I walk in His ways.

There's so many things I can do and the choice is mine,

Walking by my Father's side is where I know I'll be fine.

On this side of heaven I depend on God for everything,

For He sees all and knows what this life can bring.

As He directs my path I know I can always trust Him,

And He has proven this to me time and again.

On this side of heaven I always want more,

Of the wonderful blessings my heavenly Father has in store.

I want peace, love and, joy for everyone in their life,

No more sickness or worries I want everything to be all right.

On this side of heaven where my life begin,

Is the promise from God that we will one day live with Him?

Where the sun always shines as we bask in His glory,

On the other side of heaven with a new journey and story.

Only The Best

Only the best I heard God softly say,

For the sins of my children as Jesus died for us that day.

Only the best did God truly give,

So we could be forgiven and enjoy this life that we live.

Only the best because God loves us so much,

Knowing we could never repay what Jesus done for us.

Only the best it's so hard to believe,

All the things that my heavenly Father has done for me.

Only the best of everything comes from Him,

True compassion, and mercy and love that never ends.

Only the best is what He sees in me,

His child who is so unworthy how can this be?

Only the best I pray I always give,

To my Father who I love every day that I live.

Our Love

It was the spring of our lives when we fell in love,

And it felt like we were soaring on the wings of a dove.

Everything was exciting and so brand new,

There never could be no one else for me but you.

And summer time came and our love was growing strong,

Perfect in every way I knew nothing could go wrong.

We were so very happy no worries or cares,

We talked for hours we had so much to share.

Fall was approaching bringing so many things,

We had children to raise and things started to change.

There were bills to pay and jobs needing done,

Our love just grew stronger for we truly were one.

Winter was approaching and the children were raised,

We both had grown older our love entered another phase.

Now just the two of us together again,

With love I'm so grateful to be with my best friend.

Holding hands as we walk or sitting in our favorite chairs,

Looking back at our lives we have so much we've shared.

Oh the seasons of our love filled with so many good things,

God is so good and I know we will have another spring.

Out of The Fire

Having comfort and wealth, and everything that we need,

Doesn't give God the chance to plant His loving seeds.

Learning to love and to be grateful for everything,

Comes from heartaches and pain that this life sometimes brings.

Giving God the chance to reach out and help you,

Allowing Him to take over when you don't know what to do.

All the wealth in this world, and the fame and the glory,

Can never compare to adversities gripping stories.

For out of the fire, and the suffering and tears,

Comes the sweetest stories that everyone wants to hear.

The greatest people ever known, and the lives that are blessed,

Are the ones that have had problems, and been put to the test?

Broken lives, shattered dreams, God loves us just as we are,

For He knows what we will be when we come out of the fire.

Out Of The way

Out of the way goes our trials, and troubles and fears,

Because our heavenly Father who loves us is near.

Out of the way goes our heartaches, and sadness too,

Because our Father is on His way to take care of me and you.

Out of the way goes every sickness, and pain in our life,

For just one touch from Gods healing hand, makes everything all right.

Out of the way goes the senseless killings, and hate for one another,

For our Savior's coming back, and in peace we'll all live together.

Out of the way goes the crime, and the greed so many have,

For with God their wants will change, and they'll be happy instead of sad.

Out of the way goes the abuse, and the violence everywhere,

For our heavenly Father is showing us, how to love and to care.

Out of the way goes the temptations that leads us to sin,

For with Gods love in our hearts we will want to follow Him.

Out of the way in this life, goes all the things that we don't want or need,

For with love God created us, and He is planting so many seeds.

Out of the way God goes for all of us, each and every day,

Open your hearts the time has come, we need to walk in His ways.

Pouring Out my Heart

Dear God I come to you today,

Pouring out my heart in every way.

Sometimes the road seems so hard to walk,

I just need to sit with you and talk.

I know you listen and you understand,

For you love me and care about who I am.

I love it when I feel so close to you,

And I know that's where you want me too.

Right by your side walking with you each day,

As you listen to the things I have to say.

I have so much that I am so grateful for,

And you just keep on blessing me more.

And on the days when I'm feeling down,

I can always look up because you're around.

 I'm so humbled and blessed by everything that you do,

And I pray that you know how much I love you,

You're my comfort my joy, and the peace that I need.

The one who always listens as I pour my heart out to thee.

Praising God

I love the light of Gods morning glory as I start each day,

He gives me a song down in my heart to sing along my way.

I look up instead of looking down all because God took the time,

To share His mercy and His grace, and change this life of mine.

I love the peace that fills my soul and helps me understand,

 I have so much to look forward to for my life He has a plan.

I am so blessed with all I have from my Father up above,

Who always shines His light on me and does it with His love.

I am filled with joy and happiness on this road I trod,

Forever grateful I'm on my way while always praising God.

Pray For Us Daddy

Pray for us daddy we need Jesus in every way,

We been praying for you daddy each and every day.

Something is going wrong and we are really scared,

Daddy do you still love us we need you to show us you care.

You always tell us to say our prayers and everything will be ok,

Daddy we been praying, are we saying them the wrong way?

I don't think Jesus is listening maybe it's because we are so young,

Because daddy you keep doing the same things when you tell us you are done.

Sometimes you get so mean and your voice gets really loud.

We lost our home and everything and you want us to make you proud.

Daddy we are trying but sometimes you are hard to love,

We really need you to pray daddy to Jesus up above.

Mommy says you have a choice and there's help for what you do,

Daddy we didn't ask to be born but were here and we need you.

We don't want to lose you daddy but we feel like we've already lost,

You really need to talk to Jesus He understands cause He suffered on the cross.

If this is the way you want to live you know we will still love you,

But it makes us cry and mommy is sad because she loves you too.

Please pray for us daddy our whole world is falling apart,

Remember you're the one who told us Jesus loves you with all of His heart.

Raggedy Ann's and Ugly Ducklings

An angel quietly approached God one day,

Asking Him if He had seen some of the people He had made.

Some are beautiful some are ok and some are even grand,

But God have you seen the Ugly Ducklings and Raggedy Ann's?

God smiled and looked at her as He replied "you're questioning me"?

Looking through your eyes you will never be able to see what I can see.

Those Raggedy Ann's and ugly ducklings were perfectly made,

They've been tossed aside and mistreated in so many ways.

They are the ones who have so much compassion and love,

Always reaching out to someone else sharing my hope from above.

It doesn't take much to make them happy to them a little is a lot,

They are always thanking me for everything in life that they got.

These are the ones who knows the true meaning of what it is to trust,

They rely on me their heavenly Father who loves them so much.

Raggedy Ann's and ugly ducklings are teaching the world so much today,

About faith hope, and love, and why its so important to always pray.

As God sat back He smiled and asked the angel to look again,

She saw so much beauty the kind that can only begin with in.

For every Raggedy Ann, and Ugly Duckling God has a special plan,

As their beauty shines so bright for they've been touched by the Masters hand

Remember Me Always

Remember me always Jesus whispered to me,

Trust me in the things that you don't always see.

Know that I am with you wherever you are,

Follow your dreams with me you can go far.

Remember me always have faith in who I am,

I suffered and died on the cross for your sins.

I'm your rainbow after the storms that always goes away,

And your strength when you need it to get through your day.

Remember me always in everything that you do,

For I'm the one who really cares and truly loves you.

I'm the hope that you need when you want to give up,

And the drink when you thirst for that heavenly cup.

Remember me always when you want to stray,

Talk to me for I hear every prayer that you pray.

I'm the answer that you have been searching for,

Have faith for I can open so many doors.

Remember me always I heard it again,

With love in my heart I could never forget Him.

Remind Me

Dear God when I get so caught up in everything,

That takes my peace and joy that you bring.

And I let my worries and all my fears,

Consume me like they have down through the years.

When my days seem long and my nights never end,

And I ask myself where I even begin.

When my thoughts sometimes just come and go,

And I keep searching for answers that only you know.

I pray dear God that you take my hand,

And remind me that you are always with me again.

That every step that I take and the air that I breath,

I can do because of how much you love me.

Remind me dear God of everything that I have,

And with you I can make it when times seem bad.

That this too shall pass please let me see,

Because I have you to always remind me.

Settle Me Down Lord

Settle me down Lord as only you can,

I need a touch from your healing hand.

My worries are many and my good days are few,

Help me to remember that I always have you.

Show me all the things Lord that I need to see,

Especially the things you want me to leave be.

Cover me with your comfort, and hold me close by your side,

For it is in your love Lord I pray I always abide.

Carry me when I'm weak Lord and feel like I can't stand,

Remind me of all your promises, and all of your plans.

Help me to see all the good things in my life every day,

And to give all my problems to you when I pray.

Fill my heart with happiness, and every good thing from you,

Showing me just how much you want me to be happy too.

Settle me down Lord in your own special way,

Reassuring me that with you everything will be ok.

So Many Prayers God

There are so many prayers God always coming your way,

And you take the time to listen and answer each one every day.

Lots of prayers from mothers who are so worried about their kids,

And fathers down on their knees praying for a job and a place to live.

Farmers out in their fields that are dry praying for some rain to come,

And you keep right on answering showing everyone that you're not done.

Prayers for loved ones and friends who are sick needing your healing touch,

And there you are in their room with them because you love them so much.

There are children praying for their parents and for their lives to get better,

And you hold them close promising you will love and be with them forever.

Prayers from so many who are getting older and need you're helping hand,

Looking up there you are God always ready to reach out and help again.

There are so many prayers being lifted up to you from all walks of life,

And everyone to you is special and only you can make everything alright.

So many prayers God and you never ever take the time to rest,

For you love us so much and always give us your best.

That Nobody

That nobody to you is somebody to God,

Who walks by their side down every road that they trod.

Created out of love they are so special to Him,

They are daughters, and sons, and to so many friends.

Loved by their families and so special in every way,

Something you would see if you just talked to them one day.

From that nobody you can learn so many things,

How to share happiness and joy instead of the heartache you bring.

Everyone needs love and yes that includes you,

But real love you won't find in the things that you do.

That nobody you bully in so many ways,

Might be the one that you need in your life one day.

Right now you feel big and even strong,

But in your heart God is telling you this is so wrong.

One day you will regret all the things you have done,

The hurt and the pain that you caused someone.

There is so many things you can never take back,

Before it's too late stop and get your life on the right track.

That nobody is someone just different from you,

Who wishes that one day you could walk in their shoes.

The Breath Of Life

The breath of life God gave to me,

From the day that I was first conceived.

Waiting where I was safe and warm,

To be held one day in loving arms.

Welcomed with love by everyone,

Would it be a daughter or a son?

It mattered not to God above,

Who created me out of His love.

For He alone already knew,

Before He sent me down to you.

My destiny my life and plans,

Laid out for me by the Great I Am.

A gift from God to be loved and treasured,

A new life whose value could never be measured.

The breath of life God gave to me,

So wanted and so loved by my family.

The Great Physician

"Come to me," He softly whispered in my ear,

It was the great Physician who calmed all my fears.

"Take my hand and let's just walk awhile,

I know your needs for you are my child.

I see you struggle every day,

Calling out my name every time you pray.

You wonder if I'm even listening to you,

My child, I'm the one who knows what to do.

Your healing may not happen in a day,

For there are things that I want you to learn along the way.

I need you to trust and to understand,

That, for your life, I have a plan.

There will be sunshine but not every day,

And these are the times that you will come to me and pray.

That the skies, they are not always blue,

But you will see that I will always take care of you.

You'll begin to share my joy and my love,

Telling others about your Father up above.

And how much that I have done for you,

Knowing that the great Physician will see you through."

The Master's Garden

He picked the right spot in every way,

As He began to plant His perfect garden that day.

There were so many things that would bloom there,

He would tend it with all of His love and care.

Every flower would be beautiful selected by Him,

And He would water it with faith when He began.

He knew they would all grow so differently,

And their beauty would show for all to see.

He made sure that the Son would shine every day,

Helping His flowers to grow in their own special way.

There was all different colors different kinds and blooms,

For in the masters garden there was plenty of room.

When the rain would come down from up above,

It would shower His garden with mercy and love.

And the Son would provide everything that they'd need,

For the master with love had planted every seed.

The master tends to His garden night and day,

Knowing every flower has a place in His beautiful bouquet.

The Package

I received a package and I offered to pay,

But it was free, and thank you was all I could say.

It was not fancy there were no pretty bows.

I wondered what was inside I really wanted to know.

There was no return address it was mine to keep,

When I opened it up I began to weep.

There was so many things and I needed them all,

I looked up towards the heavens, and on God's name I called.

There was mercy and grace, and forgiveness inside,

I fell on my knees and I began to cry.

It didn't stop there it was full of love,

Sent down to me from my Father above.

There was comfort and, strength to get me through my bad days,

And lots of faith and hope, showing me God was the only way.

There was compassion and kindness, I now had so much to share,

All because of my Father who loves me and cares.

There was so many things this package never would end,

It was mine to keep forever and use over again.

I knew where to keep it as I opened my heart,

This package what a blessing that gave my life a new start.

The People Who Loves Them

Dear God it's so hard to watch every day,

The ones that we love struggle in so many ways.

Knowing their battles not over and that they may not win,

It breaks our hearts as we pray for the bad times to end.

Wishing so badly that there was more we could do,

Down on our knees we bring our loved ones to you.

You are the 'way maker' God and you always will be,

Taking care of us all seeing the things that we don't see.

We want their lives to be better and we want it today,

But your timing is not ours and you do things your way.

In life there will always be some things we don't understand,

Things that are not always a part of your plans.

Only you dear God knows the end of their story,

You can take all their bad times and turn them into glory.

With love in our hearts God we thank you again,

For your comfort, and strength for the people who loves them.

The Pieces Of My Life

Looking back at the pieces of my life there is so much that I see,

I always see my Fathers hand print on every piece that belongs to me.

On the fragile pieces God gently works and slowly takes His time,

As He puts them back together while working on this life of mine.

And the pieces that are scared and torn from the life that I have lived,

God softly soothes out every one there is so much to me He gives.

The broken pieces that in my heart I know are way beyond repair,

He takes the time to fix each one because He loves me and He cares.

The pieces that are covered in pain and the many tears I've cried,

All came together with Gods compassion who is always by my side.

And the pieces that were full of worries and fears that I did not need,

With His strength and love He fixed them all for they did not belong to me.

The pieces of my life there are so many that makes up who I am,

And I never want to forget the ones filled with joy and laughter from Him.

With His loving hands God picks me up and puts each piece back in place,

All because I am His child He truly loves that will forever have His grace.

The Rose

The rose was just a tiny bud,

Sent down to us from God above.

And slowly it began to grow,

What it would be we did not know.

The petals opened one by one,

And as they did God's will was done.

There was so much beauty we began to see,

And we realized this rose was blessing me.

Lives were being touched and filled with love,

This rose truly was a gift from God above.

People watched and waited every day,

They needed this rose in every way.

Never again would their lives be the same,

Because of this beautiful rose they now were changed.

Forever thanking God for what He had done,

Sending us this beautiful rose His only Son.

There Will Be More

There will be more of Gods blessings flowing from heaven today,

And there will be more Prayers answered when we take time to pray.

There will be more hearts mended that are broken in two,

And there will be more love for everyone sent down from God to you.

There will be more days to celebrate all the things God has for us,

And there will be more people seeing that in God they can truly trust.

There will be more joy and happiness where there once was none,

And there will be more people giving praise thanking God for what He's done.

There will be more lives filled with hope as they look to God up above,

And there will be more that are so grateful for His unfailing love.

There will be more that will begin to truly understand,

God's word as it was written the road map to His plans.

They Will Be Surprised

This world is so full of corruption and sin,

They will all be surprised when Jesus comes back again.

The ones that don't worship, trust Him, or believe,

Will bow down on their knees when they see Him, and grieve.

All of those years when they had the time,

Denied He was real thinking what they believed was fine.

Some of them even thought that He was dead,

Overlooking the Bible, just another book to be read.

Only caring about themselves and the life that they lived,

Never taking the time, to enjoy all that God had to give.

Thinking that they were the really smart ones,

How sad that their lives did not include Jesus God's Son.

One day when God returns He will split open the skies,

Some will rejoice and be happy, while others will be surprised.

TO YOU

To you I may seem very small, I'm not that big at all,

But swallow me or crush me up with one big snort you'll fall.

You love me more than anything I've taken over your life,

I'm all you want, all that you need, I'm on your mind from morning till night.

Forget your kids, forget your job, forget your family,

All that they do is stand in your way, remember I'm all you need.

I'll take you places you've never been, maybe even to your grave,

I'll make you weak till you can't stand so don't even say you're brave.

I will trick you, con you, tempt you, I'll even use your friends,

Just one more pill, just one more high, come on let the good times begin.

Your family will stand by and watch, feeling helpless in every way,

The one they love is tearing them apart, they feel the pain each day.

They'll go to God, get on their knees and for you shed many tears,

They will ask, "Dear God, how long can this last?

The days have turned to years."

Just one more pill, just one more snort, who cares if God can see,

Don't worry about the tears that He has shed trying to get you away from me.

His love is strong we'll have to fight, you need to turn your back on Him,

He will never leave you, nor forsake you there's no battle He can't win.

Now don't you dare get weak on me and run back to your Father!

With all God's strength and power, why should I even bother?

For every life, God has a plan, all you need to do is follow,

Maybe I'm not really what you need, I'll leave you feeling hollow.

The choice is yours, you get to choose we only have one life,

To love our kids and family, follow God and do what's right.

Turn Around

Oh what a blessing a new baby's been born,

Now being held by their mother so soft and so warm.

Wrapped up in a blanket as they travel home,

So loved and so wanted they'll never be alone.

Turn around and their talking as they run and play,

It seems like they were so small just yesterday.

Now off to school as mom wave's goodbye,

Turning to leave with tears in her eyes.

Turn around and the teen years are already here,

As they travel out in the big world mom's heart fills with fear.

Praying for she knows God will watch over them,

What would she do if she didn't have Him.

Turn around college is over their getting married next week,

So happy and in love again moms heart skips a beat.

Trusting God for only He can be with them all the time,

Forever grateful mom thanks Him for she knows they'll be fine.

Turn around there is grandkids and joy everywhere,

As grandma laughs and plays without any cares.

Thanking God up above for her life is complete,

As she kisses her loved ones so precious and sweet.

Turnaround time is going by way to fast,

The grandkids are grown and on their own at last.

Again grandma prays for Gods loving grace,

Knowing He will see them through everything that they face.

Turn around mom is reminded as she looks in the mirror,

That life is a journey and it doesn't end here.

Looking up towards the heavens praising God every day,

With footsteps that are slower she still walks in His ways.

Under The Rainbow

Under the rainbow where the children all play,

Safe in God's love and mercy all day.

Singing so happy no worries or cares,

Enjoying their life so thankful their there.

Holding hands with each other with smiles on their face,

Knowing in their hearts nothing could ever take Gods place.

Looking up at the beautiful colors, loving every one,

Grateful in their hearts for what their Father has done.

Always taking the time to stop and to see,

All the beautiful things saying God made this for me.

Lots of laughter and giggles and never no doubts,

Trusting God to take care of things they know nothing about.

What a wonderful blessing God wants us to see,

Through the eyes of the children how happy we can be.

Under the rainbow I want to go every day,

And learn from the children as I watch them run and play.

Unfinished

Unfinished our lives are in so many ways,

Still being molded by our Savior every day.

Unfinished changes that only He can do,

Changes that will bring happiness to me and to you.

Broken pieces needing fixed that we don't understand,

Until we see them put back together by our Saviors healing hands.

Unfinished business this world we live in has so much,

Down on our knees we pray for God's healing touch.

So many lives that are lost searching for hope every day,

Needing to look up to the one who will show us the way.

Forever blessed, forever loved His promises are true,

No matter where we are or what we need, God will take care of you.

It is finished God cried out as Jesus died on the cross,

A new beginning for everyone as His Son paid the cost.

Unfinished there's so many things we see as we look around,

Thanking God we are so grateful we know where the finisher can be found.

Up The Mountain

I went up to the mountain was I ready to climb?

And leave all my sorrows and heartaches behind.

The climb was not easy the road was not smooth,

But I knew in my heart this was something I needed to do.

One step at a time with God leading the way,

The climb would get easier with each passing day.

There were rocks to climb over the path was so steep,

Tears fell from my eyes as I started to weep.

I was so scared I wouldn't make it and fear filled my mind,

When I felt my heavenly Father draw me closer saying you will be fine.

I climbed on through the rough spots with thorns scratching me,

And I finally started noticing the things God wanted me to see.

I saw flowers that were blooming so beautiful to my sight.

And there were stars always shining even on my darkest nights.

There was a peace that filled my soul and so much love in my heart,

And so many things that I had longed for right from the start.

I saw a light that was shining brightly through the trees,

I felt Gods warmth as I realized this light was shining on me.

I was so grateful as I climbed getting closer to the top,

That my Father was always with me His love never stops.

Holding His Hand I'll keep climbing with someone who loves me,

My life is so blessed and I have so much I now see.

Walk With Me Jesus

Walk with me Jesus hold on to my hand,

Can we talk about my life and what you have planned?

Walk with me Jesus I get so afraid,

I need to know that you are with me every day.

Walk with me Jesus when I feel so alone,

Letting me know that I am your own.

Walk with me Jesus when I get so tired,

Showing me that with you life isn't always this hard.

Walk with me Jesus through every trial,

As you take time to show me they only last for a little while.

Walk with me Jesus whenever I cry,

While holding me close as you wipe the tears from my eyes.

Walk with me Jesus there's so much I want to know,

And the only way I can learn is if in your direction I go.

Walk with me Jesus I love our time together,

As you softly whisper my child I'll walk with you forever.

WE ARE

We are the hope that someone might need,

Leading them to the light that helps them to see.

We are the strength that can help them get up,

Reaching out with a helping hand that they need so much.

We are the ones who can help mold their dreams,

Showing them that with God nothings impossible it seems.

We are the voice that God uses each day,

To touch and encourage someone in every way.

We are the ones whose lives have been blessed,

Because of our Father we can share so much happiness.

We are the reason God sacrificed His only Son,

Letting others know that Jesus is the saving one.

We can say the prayers that so many need,

Grateful that our Father always answers and intercedes.

We all touch each other's hearts in so many ways,

Sharing God's love with someone who needs it today.

We Never Know

We never know someone else's pain or where they might have been,

But with love in our hearts and everything we have we need to pray for them.

We never know the hope they've lost their defeat and their despair,

But God gives us the chance to reach out and let them know we care.

We never know the road they've walked or how many times they've failed,

But with compassion we can take the time to listen, to their story only they can tell.

We never know how alone they feel or how afraid that they might be,

But with God's help we can talk to them about the things that they might need.

We never know when they wake each day the worries that's on their mind,

But we can pray and tell them about God, being patient for some things take time.

We never know what's in their hearts but God our Father does,

And He gives us the chance to always reach out and show them they are loved.

We never know so many things but God has shown us that we can trust,

That in His time things will get better, and we are blessed when He uses us.

What God Sees

There are things in life that saddens you and me,

But it cannot compare to all that God sees.

God see's the whole world and everyone,

All the pain and destruction to lives that is done.

All the heartache and sorrows He see's day and night,

God does not take a rest for were never out of His sight.

I wonder how many times that His heart must break,

For the things that we chose and the choices we make.

Does He shed a tear does it make Him cry?

He knows all the answers so He never asks why.

When I think of all He sees and does,

It reminds me of just how much He loves.

And all the sacrifices that He has made,

So that we can live with Him someday.

There has been so many times that He protects us all,

I'm so grateful to Him that on His name I can call.

Knowing that He will always take care of me,

And shield me from the things that only His eyes see.

What God's Love Does

God's love calms me when I'm afraid and worried all of the time,

Letting me know that He is always there and with Him I will be fine.

God's love fills me with lots of hope that lets me dream each day,

Showing me with Him all things are possible and He will make a way.

God's love gives me peace that I sometimes need when I don't understand,

While He takes the time to let me know that this too is a part of His plan.

God's love guides my life and keeps me safe from the things that would do me harm,

As He holds me closely by His side protecting me in His loving arms.

God's love covers me through every storm that comes into my life,

Showing me that I will be ok as He makes everything alright.

God's love has everything in life I need and to Him I always go,

He answers every prayer that I pray for everything He knows.

God's love for me goes so far beyond and to it there is no end,

With His loving hands He created me and it was with love that I began.

What Gods Love Looks Like

What does Gods love look like, well let me see,

I can only share what it looks like to me.

I see it when I look up and the suns shining bright,

And I see it in the stars and the moon that lights up the night.

It is in the hearts of those that love Him so much,

I've seen it when so many have been blessed by His touch.

I see it in the hope that He places in everyone's heart,

When they feel like their world is falling apart.

What does Gods love look like it's all over the place?

I've seen it in His mercy and forgiveness, and grace.

And in the hand that reaches out to their fellowman,

As they share Gods love with everyone that they can.

I've seen it when the doctors give up with no cure in sight,

And a miracle happens because Gods love made things right.

I have seen it and I've felt it in so many ways,

God's love that is always with me every day.

What does Gods love look like, look around and you'll see,

And when you look in the mirror you'll see it in you, trust me.

What He Didn't Give Me

There are so many prayers sometimes that I say,

Asking you and thanking you for things every day.

When I look at my life and I'm feeling down,

There is so many good things that I have found.

What I love the most is the things that I see,

That you dear God didn't give me.

Things with no meaning that would keep me from you,

When I have needed you and did not know what to do.

A heart that is hard with no compassion inside,

Letting all the worthwhile things in life pass me by.

Thinking that the riches in this life is all that I need,

Forgetting about you not knowing what I need to succeed.

Never taking the time to enjoy all the blessings that you send,

Like the sunshine in my day, and the peaceful rest at days end.

Feeling alone like there is no hope anywhere,

Not knowing what it's like to have a Father who cares.

You are the greatest gift God and I'm so happy when I see,

All of the things in this life that you didn't give me.

What He Is

He's the top of my mountain that I have to climb,

He is my light in the darkness that for me always shines.

He's my strength when I need it and I have to be strong,

He is the wind in my sails that always pushes me along.

He's my joy every morning when I open my eyes,

He's the comfort I need every time that I cry.

He's the walk that I take when I need to calm down,

He's where I go when I'm lost and need to be found.

He's the sun that shines on me when I want to just hide,

He is the presence I feel always there by my side.

He's my answer my hope for the things I don't know,

He is the hand that holds mine and it never lets go.

He is the calm in my life when the storm rages on,

He's the birds that I love that sing me their song.

He's my Father, my God; He's everything that I need,

He's the one who I know will forever love me.

What I Cannot Do

What I cannot do I know God can,

For He created who I am.

He knows my heart and He sees my life,

He understands my sorrows and all of my strife's.

He knows what I am thinking and He intercedes,

Knowing that this trial is way too big for me.

Quietly He takes it, softly saying this is mine,

Just trust me I promise you will be fine.

Right now there is so much standing in your way,

But you struggle and you keep fighting every day.

It's a battle that on your own you will never win,

I love you so much that is why I stepped in.

You worry and you keep asking me why,

And I see the tears that falls from your eyes.

Your heart is soft and your love is deep,

Remember I'm your heavenly Father whose promises I keep.

Come to me and let me hold you for a while,

I will give you the peace, and comfort that you need now.

I will take care of all your problems in my own time,

Give them to me, and forget them, the ones you love will be fine.

Never forget just how much that I love your family to,

And that I am the life changer who can do the things you cannot do.

What Is God Doing

What is God doing He's making a way,

For the things in your life that you need every day.

The big things the small things they all matter to Him,

He's always working for your good time and again.

What is God doing He's watching over you,

Showing you no matter what He takes care of you too.

In the good times and bad times He's always there,

Because He loves you so much and He truly cares.

What is God doing He's walking by your side,

Leading you the right way He's a wonderful guide.

Hoping that you never let go of His hand,

For He is the one who knows your life plan.

What is God doing He's answering your prayers,

Listening to everything with Him that you share.

As He holds you close with His compassion and love,

Sending down His blessings from heaven above.

What is God doing whatever it is,

You are included because He loves you and you're His.

What Would I Do Lord

What would I do Lord if I didn't have you?

To guide me and help me in everything that I do.

My life would be empty and my hope would be gone,

I'd have no one to trust, I wouldn't even know right from wrong.

I'd wake up each morning with nothing to say,

If I didn't have you Lord there'd be no reason to pray.

My heart would be empty of the love that I need,

No compassion and no caring, with no one to plant the seeds.

I'd go through each day with nothing to share,

If I didn't have you Lord and you were no longer there.

My joy and happiness that truly comes from you,

Would no longer be with me Lord what would I do?

"My child without me you wouldn't even be here",

But you are and I love you I promise I'll always be near.

I created this world and most importantly you,

That's why you will never have to ask lord what would I do?

Eva Dimel
Eva's Inspirations

When I Pray

When I get down on my knees to pray,

I see God's blessings in every way.

I have a peace that passes all understanding,

And my life no longer seems so demanding.

My worries and fears slowly drift away,

Every time I get down on my knees to pray.

I can feel the son shining down on me,

And there is so many good things I now can see.

All the ones in my life that I love so much,

I know will be blessed by God's healing touch.

I have so many things I can now look forward to,

All because I took the time to give my burdens, God to you.

I am so blessed so wanted and so loved every day,

By my Father in heaven who listens when I pray.

When I

When I am weak Lord you are so strong,

And you lend me your strength to carry on.

When I am afraid Lord and full of fear,

You let me know its ok because you are here.

When I am sad Lord and all I do is cry,

You comfort me as you wipe the tears from my eyes.

When I have failed you Lord you reassure me,

That I am a work in progress and it's my heart that you see.

When I feel hopeless Lord and my trials are too tough,

You remind me I have you and to never give up.

When I need anything it's to you Lord I pray,

My Father who loves me and is with me night and day.

When God Made Me

When God dug down into the clay that day,

He made me perfect in every way.

When He was done and He took one look at me,

His heart filled with love even the angels could see.

This one might have some problems one of the angels said,

He answered this is my child and they have nothing to dread.

But I see so many things God that can go wrong.

I will carry them when they need me until they are strong.

They will fail you and at times be so full of fear,

Its ok I will hold them they'll know that I'm always here.

There's going to be times that they cry and want to give up,

I'll show them they can make it when life gets to tough.

God are you sure, they're not always going to follow your plans,

Oh I'm positive just trust me I'll give them the chance to try again.

They are going to be so blessed with all your mercy and grace,

This is my child and I'm their Father no one could ever take their place.

When Jesus Says My Name

When Jesus says my name my heart beats a little faster,

Feeling so blessed and, excited about what He is after.

I quietly listen as He softly speaks to me,

Knowing there is something that He wants me to see.

Everything around me stops and I feel so glorified,

I feel His presence for He is right there by my side.

When Jesus says my name there is so much love I feel,

My Father my Savior so precious and so real.

I humbly answer down on bended knee,

Forever grateful that Jesus is speaking to me.

When Jesus says my name peace just fills my soul,

Knowing He loves me my joy I can hardly hold.

Not one word from Him do I ever want to miss, I am so blessed that I am a child of His.

I have called on His name so many times,

But I am in awe when I hear Him whisper mine.

When Jesus says my name I feel so close to Him,

Patiently I wait knowing He will say my name again.

Always looking around not knowing when it will be,

In my heart forever thanking Him for using me.

When You Awoke

God kissed you this morning, when you awoke to a brand new day,

He put His angels all around you, as you went about your way.

He kept His healing Hands upon you, so that you could make it through,

For He loves you so much, there's nothing for you He will not do.

His light shone all around you, no matter where you went,

Rich or poor, in great big mansions, or on the roadside in a tent.

When He looks at us, He sees His children that He dearly loves,

Blessing us with Hope, and Grace sent from His home, Heaven above.

When you awoke today, God kissed you as He looked upon your face,

His precious child He loves so much, no one could ever take your place

Where I Came From

When I look back at where I came from God you always remind me I came from you,

And you take the time to let me know you love me no matter what I've been through.

There is so many things about me God that still today I don't always understand,

You reassure me it doesn't matter for the things in this world are not always your plans.

When I look back at where I came from God I realize how far I have come,

And I see so many things in my life reminding me where you've brought me from.

I have walked down so many roads sometimes feeling lost and so all alone,

And I felt you right beside me as you took my hand and led me back home.

When I look back at where I came from God I see that you was always there with me,

Through the good and the bad, without you God I don't know where I'd be.

You protected me from so many things with your love and your mercy, and grace,

Letting me know I was your child who you loved, and no one could ever take my place.

When I look back at where I came from God with so much love" I can now say from you,"

My heavenly Father who has my future planned, giving me so much to look forward too.

Where the Heart Is

They say home is where the heart is, and Lord I want my heart with you,

I have been so many places, and you have seen what my heart's been through.

My heart has been in the valleys, with trials I thought would never end,

But you Lord was always with me, there to lead me out again.

And when my heart was broken, and full of sorrow and pain,

It was you Lord who held me and showed me, that your love would always reign.

There were times that my heart was hardened, by so many things that I had seen,

And I thought that true happiness only happened, to others and in your dreams.

I have walked down many roads, and wondered if this was where I belonged,

Looking up I seen the sunshine and realized that I was wrong.

Lord you took my hand and you showed me, that home is where true love begins,

And that happiness and joy is always there, with blessings that never end.

Lord home is where my heart is and my heart belongs to you,

I'm at peace when I'm with you Lord, and my heart is filled with happiness to

Where Will You Take Me Today

My child I always follow you,

And I see everything in life that you do.

There are times that I laugh, and times that I cry,

And even though I know the answers, I still wonder why.

When I see the things that you choose to do,

Only thinking and caring about number one you.

I have held so many as they have cried,

Because they love you so much, and their afraid you will die.

I know what you will leave behind,

But those things never seem to enter your mind.

I wish that I could make you care,

About the ones who pray, and are always there.

Little children reaching out that don't understand,

They will always love you as best as they can.

They look up to you and don't know where to go,

But you my child in your heart truly know.

The path that you're on is pushing me away,

Is this what you want when with my life I paid?

So you could have a life that's good,

And do the things you know you should.

It's your choice and I'm waiting on what you will say,

Asking in my heart, where will you take me today?

I am God, I'm your Father, and it's never too late,

My arms are open for you, I have hope, and for you I'll wait.

Who Do You Go To For Comfort

Who do you go to for comfort when no one is around?

When everything in your life seems to be looking down.

Who do you go to for comfort, when you are feeling so all alone?

Needing to be loved and wanted, hoping for a place to call home.

Who do you go to for comfort and the security that you need?

Looking back down through your life, there's not a memory that you want to see.

Who do you go to for comfort for I have only found one true place?

Straight to the arms of my heavenly Father, who softly wipes the tears from my face.

Who do you go to for comfort to the one who truly loves me?

Who sacrificed His only Son Jesus, so from my sins I could be set free.

Who do you go to for comfort to my Father who is always there?

The one who has never let me down, and shows me just how much He cares.

Who do you go to for comfort, to the one who never leaves my side?

My God, my Father, my everything who gives me hope and a reason to try.

Who Loves You

Looking back at all the things in life I've been through,

With no one to trust not always knowing what to do.

Wanting to be happy and live my life normally,

As a child this is all that I ever wanted for me.

Being afraid of the dark as I suffered inside,

With no one to help me all I could do was cry.

Knowing there was a God when I went to Sunday school,

But He never lived at our house I didn't think He wanted to.

I just knew I was worthless with no value of my own,

There were so many houses we lived in but none of them was a home.

As a child I would always dream of a much better life,

With no more fighting or bad things where everyone would be all right.

Now as an adult I am living in a house that's a home,

With God by my side and my family I am never alone.

Enjoying all the blessings He pours out on me every day,

As He shows me I am His child in every way.

And at times when I think of the things I've been through,

I can hear God softly whisper "I'm here the one who loves you."

Why

Why are you crying so hard today?

Your heavenly Father is on His way.

Where is your joy and the laughter you had?

Your Father will comfort you whenever you're sad.

Why are you worried about so many things?

When your heavenly Father will take care of everything.

Who do you run to when you feel like you can't cope?

Your Father in heaven is where you will find so much hope.

Why are you searching in all the wrong places for love?

When real love comes from your Father in heaven above.

Down on your knees as you talk to Him.

He reaches out and comforts you again.

Your tears are now gone and have been replaced with a smile,

As you spend time with your Father in prayer for a while.

Looking up you now see that your cup over flows,

You're no longer asking why because you already know.

The one that you need and for you is always there,

Your heavenly Father who loves you and took on all your cares.

With God

Broken down and wondering why,

Seeking reassurance and a reason to try.

Needing the strength to try again,

Not really knowing where to begin.

Looking for answers, I want them today,

Please help me through this, Dear God, I pray.

Needing someone to hold onto,

Hearing God say "I'm here for you".

Letting me know that this to shall pass,

With God by my side, bad times won't last.

Thanks be to God for His compassion and love,

Hanging onto me always, sharing His strength from above.

Eva Dimel
Eva's Inspirations

With Your Love

With your love Lord I can do anything,

No matter what I'm going through or what the day brings.

With your love Lord there is so much that I see,

And I am so grateful for everything you've shown me.

With your love Lord I have so much to share,

For it over flows letting everyone know that you care.

With your love Lord so many lives have been touched,

And always with the things that we all need so much.

With your love Lord you answer when I call on your name,

Rich or poor, good or bad you love us all the same.

With your love Lord I don't have to fear,

And when I worry you softly whisper its ok I'm right here.

With your love Lord my life is complete,

For you have everything that so many seek.

With your love Lord I now understand,

What my purpose is and I know who I am.

With your love Lord I forever am blessed,

For you have never failed me you always give your best.

With your love Lord I have all that I need,

As I humbly thank you down on my knees.

With His Heart

With a heart filled with love, so faithful and true,

God took His time as He lovingly made you.

Making sure everything was in the right place,

Knowing His child would need plenty of grace.

He poured out His compassion for all of your life,

So you would always know with Him you'd be all right.

As He created you He knew your life had a plan,

That came from him and not one of man's.

With His heart He gave you the freedom to choose,

And with love He is watching what His child will do.

Without The Cross

Without the cross there would be no promises fulfilled and kept,

And Jesus would of never prayed in the garden and wept.

Without the cross there would be no forgiveness of our sins,

And when life was over here, we would die and it would be the end.

Without the cross we would have nothing in life to look forward to,

For it would not matter how we lived or what we'd do.

Without the cross there would be no mercy and Gods loving grace,

We would have no Savior to help us through the things in life we face.

Without the cross we would of never known how much we are loved,

By our Father who created us in heaven up above.

Without the cross we would have no reason to be happy and rejoice,

But God loved us so much, He sacrificed His only Son, for us He made that choice.

Without the cross there's so much in life that we would all lose,

But because Jesus died for our sins God gave us the right to choose.

With the cross we now can live our life for God every day,

Thank God He sent us a Savior His Son, Jesus to show us the way.

Wonderful Counselor

Wonderful counselor God of love,

My saving grace from heaven above.

Touching so many as He shows us the way,

To live our lives for Him every day.

Giving us the things He knows we will need

Forgiveness and guidance and a reason to believe.

Wonderful counselor my hope and life line,

Grateful in my heart for all of His time.

Day after day He watches over me,

I don't know how much more blessed I could be.

Wonderful counselor the one we can trust,

With love in His heart He always listens to us.

No matter where we are or what road we are on,

He lets us know to Him we belong.

Children of God is who we all are,

Thankful for our Savior the bright shining star.

Eva Dimel
Eva's Inspirations

You're Always Here

When night time comes and my day is done,

And I feel so tired, but sleep just won't come.

When my mind starts worrying and I lay awake,

And I toss and turn, wondering how much more I can take.

I gently close my eyes knowing what I need to do,

I call on your name Lord and I talk to you.

Then my worries and fears don't seem so big at all,

And everything looks better, when on your name I call.

I'm so grateful to you Lord, for always watching over me,

And for your comfort, and your love, that I never fail to see.

You are with me Dear Lord, when the sun is shining bright,

And you never leave my side, when it becomes dark and its night.

You take care of all my problems, and you calm all my fears,

Day or night you give me peace, for I know you're always here.

You Are Mine

You are mine not just anyone's,

I am your Heavenly Father, the holy one.

I created you and you are a part of me,

My child who I'll love through eternity.

I made you special you are one of a kind,

There is so many good things in you that I find.

I am always with you morning and night,

You are never ever out of my sight.

No matter what happens in your life today,

You're never alone for I am with you always.

I'll give you peace, joy and happiness,

Because you're mine, your life will be blessed.

I'll ease your worries, and calm all your fears,

I'll never let you go, for you I'm always here.

I will forgive you and all your sins I'll forget,

For Jesus paid the price for you, without any regrets.

Yes you are mine a child of the King,

So loved and so wanted more than anything

You God

I look at myself God and I am so weak, but you are so strong for me,

You have always been there to pick me up, when life's storms brings me to my knees.

You're the strength that I need to get through each day, and the rest that I need each night,

You're the hope that keeps me going, and the comfort I need for every tear that I cry.

You're the joy that fills my soul, and the happiness that some days never ends,

You're the reason that I can always look up, for you are where I begin.

My God, you are my everything! There is so much for me that you do,

You're the peace in my soul and the love in my heart, I'm so blessed because I belong to you

You Stood Beside Me

You stood beside me through thick and thin,

You gave me guidance when I didn't know where to begin.

You gave me comfort and wiped away my tears,

You've never left me down through the years.

You carried me when I could not walk,

You were my voice when I could not talk.

You always made a way for me,

If it wasn't for you, where would I be?

Your forgiveness makes everything all right,

Your love is with me day and night.

My loving Father, my Savior, my very best friend,

Thank you for your blessings that never end.

www.ingramcontent.com/pod-product-compliance
Lightning Source LLC
Chambersburg PA
CBHW060821050426
42453CB00008B/530